MUSICAL
INSTRUMENTS
OF THE WORLD

Drums

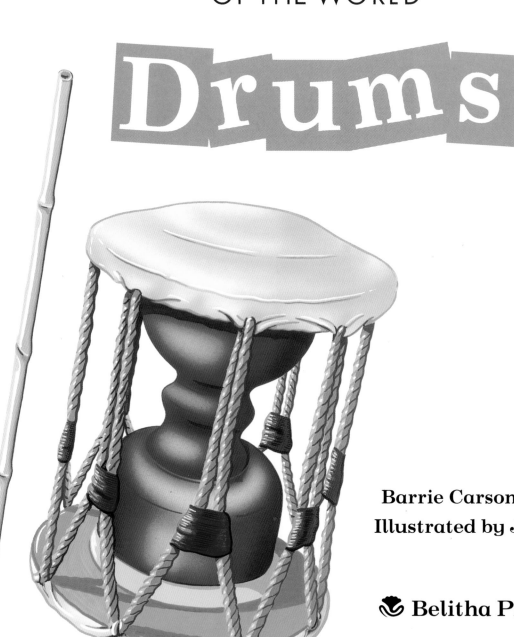

Barrie Carson Turner
Illustrated by John See

❀ Belitha Press

First published in the UK in 2000 by
Belitha Press Limited
London House, Great Eastern Wharf
Parkgate Road, London SW11 4NQ

Editor: Russell McLean
Designer: Zoe Quayle
Picture researcher: Juliet Duff
Educational consultant: Celia Pardaens

ISBN 1 84138 114 4

Printed in Singapore

British Library Cataloguing in Publication Data
for this book is available from the British Library.

10 9 8 7 6 5 4 3 2 1

Picture acknowledgements:
Andes Press Agency: 18 C & D Hill; 8, 20, 24, 28 Carlos Reyes-Manzo.
Arena Images: 29. Ffotograff: 15, 22 Patricia Aithie. Hutchison Library:
19 J.G.Fuller. Lebrecht Collection: 7, 17 Frederick Norohna; 6 Graham
Salter. London Features International: 11 David Fisher. Magnum Photos:
4-5, 26 Abbas. Panos Pictures: 12 James Bedding; 9 Sean Sprague.
Performing Arts Library: 21 Clive Barda. Redferns: 14 Odile Noel;
16, 27 David Redfern. Tony Stone Images: 23 Karen Su.

Contents

Musical

Musical instruments are played in every country of the world. There are thousands of different instruments, of all shapes and sizes. They are often divided into four groups: strings, brass, percussion and woodwind.

Percussion instruments are struck (hit), shaken or scraped to make their sound. Brass and woodwind instruments are blown to make their sound. String instruments make a sound when their strings vibrate.

instruments

This book is about drums, which are important members of the percussion group. Most drums are hollow, and have a tight skin. They are beaten with the hands or with sticks. There are many different shapes of drum. Hourglass drums are shaped like an egg timer. Goblet drums are shaped like a wine glass. Other drums are shaped like barrels, cones or tubes.

For this book we have chosen 21 drums from around the world. There is a picture of each instrument and a photograph of it being played. On pages 30 and 31 you will find a list of useful words to help you understand more about music.

Snare drum

The snare drum was originally used to give signals on a battlefield. It has two heads, or skins, one at each end of the drum. These are made of animal skin or plastic. Metal wires called snares rest against the lower head. They rattle when the drum is struck. The snare drum is sometimes called the side drum, because in marching bands players carry it at their side.

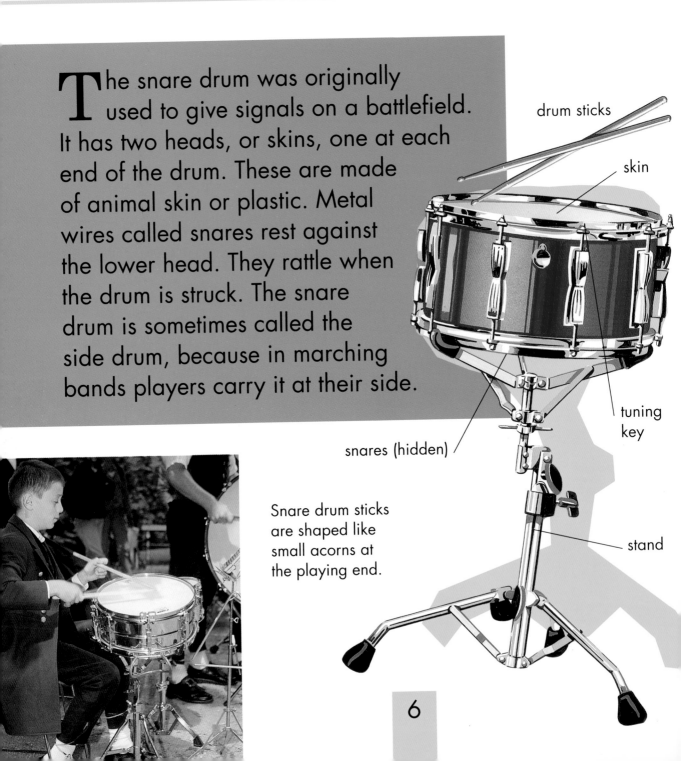

drum sticks

skin

tuning key

snares (hidden)

stand

Snare drum sticks are shaped like small acorns at the playing end.

6

Tasha

The tasha is from India. It looks like a miniature version of an orchestral drum, and hangs by a strap around the neck. The drum is made of wood, pottery or metal, and is played with bamboo sticks. The tasha is a member of the kettledrum family.

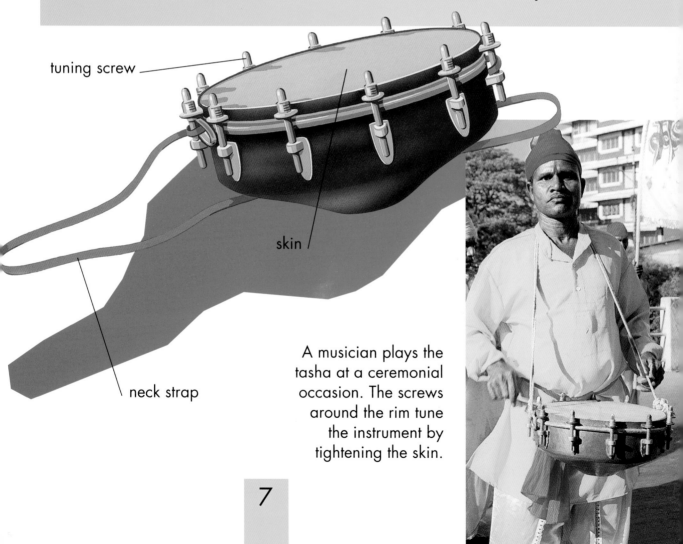

tuning screw

skin

neck strap

A musician plays the tasha at a ceremonial occasion. The screws around the rim tune the instrument by tightening the skin.

Tambour

The tambour is one of the oldest and simplest of drums. The head of the drum is made of animal skin or plastic. This is stretched over a wooden hoop called the frame. Nails hold the skin tightly in position. The tambour is a member of the frame drum family.

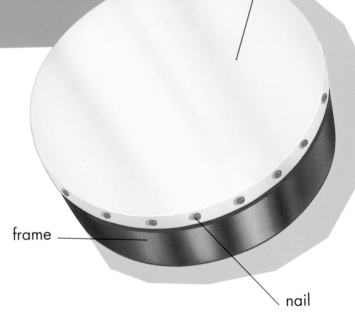

skin

frame

nail

The tambour is played with a soft drum stick, or with the fingers of one hand.

Conga drum

skin

Tuning screw

The conga drum is played with the heel and fingers of both hands. (The heel is the part of the palm near the wrist.) Players also press the skin of the drum with their elbow or wrist. This makes it sound higher. The conga drum rests on a stand or is held between the knees.

The body of the conga drum is barrel shaped. The drum is an important rhythm instrument in Latin American dance music.

Tom - toms

Tom-toms were first played in the Caribbean hundreds of years ago. European visitors gave them the name tom-tom, after the sound they made.

You are most likely to see tom-toms in a band, as part of a drum kit. Here they are played with hard wooden sticks which produce a powerful sound. Sometimes tom-toms are played in an orchestra too.

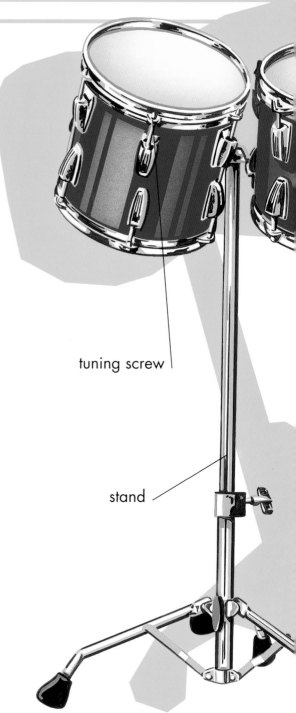

tuning screw

stand

skin

Each drum has two heads. They are usually made of plastic. The tuning screws at the top and the bottom of the drum are used to tighten the skins. Both skins must be kept tight to produce the best sound.

drum sticks

There are always at least three tom-toms in a drum kit. The two smallest tom-toms share a stand with the bass drum.

11

Bongos

Bongos are always played in pairs. Two different-sized drums are joined together by a brace. The large drum sounds low notes and the small drum sounds high notes.

The instrument is held between the knees, with the large drum always on the player's right. The drums are played with the fingers and thumb, as well as with the whole hand.

tuning screw

skin

brace

Bongos are a very important instrument in Latin American dance music. They were first played in Cuba about one hundred years ago. The bodies of early bongos were carved from tree trunks.

Good bongo playing requires great skill. Here a bongo player accompanies a solo flute player, or flautist.

13

Bodhran

The bodhran (bor-aan) is a frame drum from Ireland. It looks like a tambourine without jingles. The skin is stretched across a wooden frame shaped like a hoop. The bodhran is played with the fingers of the right hand, or with a double-headed drum stick.

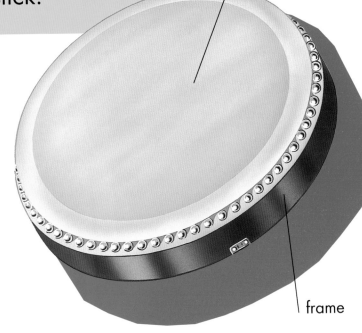

skin

frame

The bodhran is held in the left hand by rope, sticks or wires stretched across the inside of the frame.

Ingungu

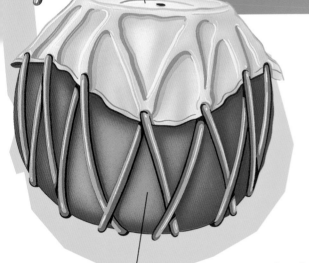

friction
stick

skin

clay pot

The ingungu is an African friction drum. It is not beaten like an ordinary drum. Drummers wet their hands before playing. Then they place the end of a thin stick or reed against the skin, and pull their hands down the stick. The friction makes vibrations. These pass from the stick into the drum, and produce a dull roaring sound.

This friction drum is easy to hold because the stick is attached to the drum skin.

Timbales

drum sticks

Timbales are from South America. They are often used in dance bands. The drums are played with thin sticks. They produce a bright, clear sound. You usually see timbales in sets of two, with one large drum and one smaller drum.

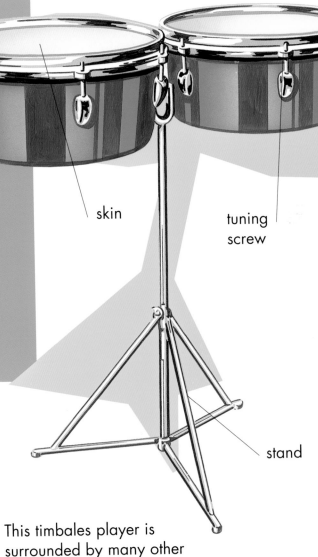

skin

tuning screw

stand

This timbales player is surrounded by many other percussion instruments, such as cowbells and conga drums.

16

Pakhavaj

The pakhavaj (puck-waaj) is from India. It has two skins, one at each end. These are laced together with a long leather strap. Corks pushed in between the straps keep the skins tight, so that the drum makes a good sound. The body of the pakhavaj is made of wood, and the heads from goatskin. Drummers hold their hands flat as they play.

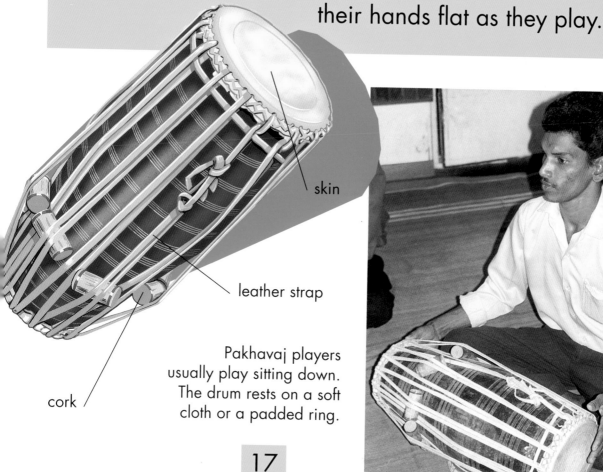

skin

leather strap

cork

Pakhavaj players usually play sitting down. The drum rests on a soft cloth or a padded ring.

Kakko

The kakko is from Japan. The body of the drum is barrel shaped. The drum heads are made of deer skin, and are fixed to large iron hoops at each end. The kakko holds the rhythm in a Japanese orchestra. The drum rests on a stand in front of the player.

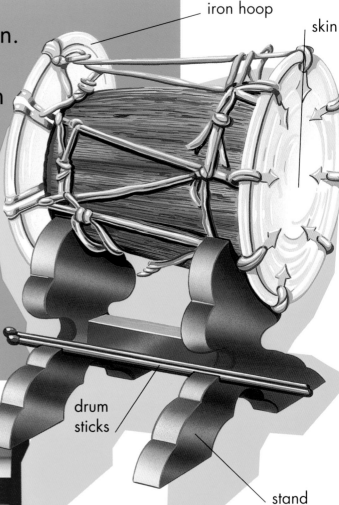

iron hoop

skin

drum sticks

stand

This musician holds the kakko steady with one hand. He strikes the drum with the other hand.

Changgo

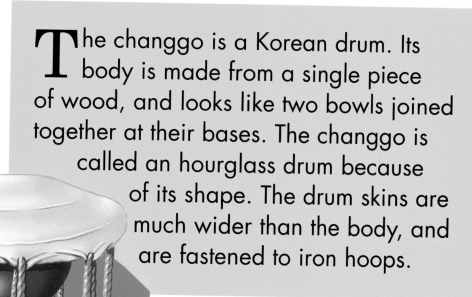

bamboo
drum stick

skin

The changgo is a Korean drum. Its body is made from a single piece of wood, and looks like two bowls joined together at their bases. The changgo is called an hourglass drum because of its shape. The drum skins are much wider than the body, and are fastened to iron hoops.

hourglass-
shaped body

iron hoop

The changgo is usually played sitting down, but in this procession the players carry their drums.

Darabukka

The darabukka is a goblet drum from North Africa and the Middle East. It can be made of wood, pottery or metal. Players hold it under their arm or rest it on their leg. The darabukka in our illustration is from Iran, where it is called a dombak.

These goblet drums are called djembes. They hang from neck straps so they can be played standing up.

skin

goblet-
shaped
body

20

Bass drum

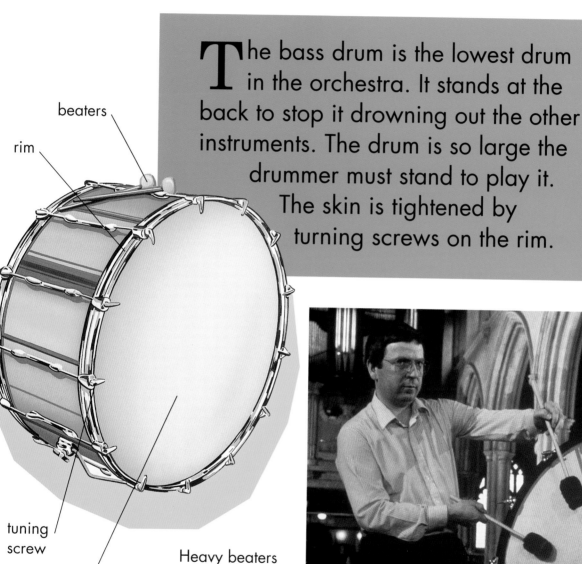

The bass drum is the lowest drum in the orchestra. It stands at the back to stop it drowning out the other instruments. The drum is so large the drummer must stand to play it. The skin is tightened by turning screws on the rim.

beaters

rim

tuning screw

skin

Heavy beaters are needed to produce the deep sound of the bass drum.

Damaru

The damaru is from Pakistan and India. It is a pellet drum with an hourglass-shaped body. When the drum is shaken from side to side, pellets strike the skins to make a loud rattling sound. Black tuning paste is smeared on to each head. This improves the sound of the drum.

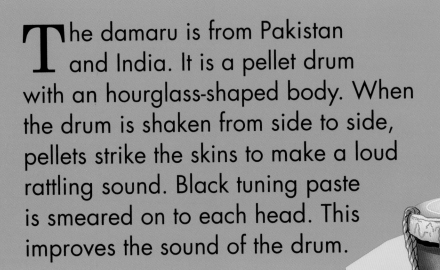

skin

tuning paste

hourglass-shaped body

pellet

This boy is playing a simple pellet drum. Pellet drums are sometimes called rattle drums or clapper drums.

22

The Chinese word for drum is gu. Most Chinese drums are shaped like flat barrels. Their shape has not changed for hundreds of years. The top skin is struck with beaters, but the bottom skin is never played. The drums are often brightly coloured and decorated with beautiful patterns.

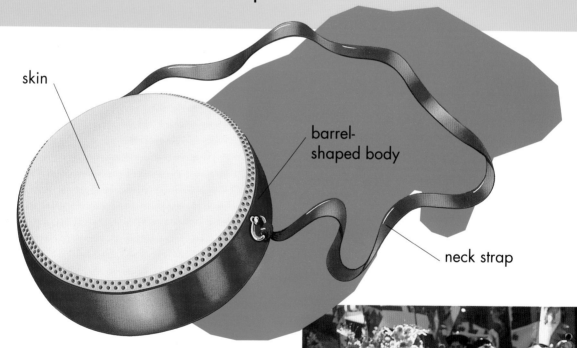

skin

barrel-shaped body

neck strap

These colourful gu players are performing at a New Year celebration.

23

Slit drum

The slit drum is not a true drum because it has no skin, but in many ways it works like a drum. A piece of wood is hollowed out, leaving one or two long slits in the top. The slits allow the sound from inside the drum to escape.

slit

These Nigerian drummers are accompanying dancers. The large slit drum on the left needs an extra large beater to give a powerful sound.

The first slit drums were carved from tree trunks thousands of years ago. To make them sound they were beaten with sticks or stamped on. Sometimes they were placed over pits in the ground to make them sound louder. Large slit drums are so loud that they can be used to send messages over long distances.

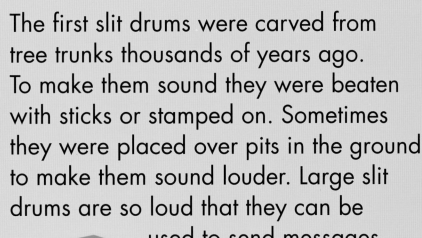

hollow inside

beater

Duff

The duff is an unusual drum because it is square. It is very light, so it can be held easily in one hand and played with the other. Sometimes it is held in both hands and played with the fingers. Some duffs contain dried beans like a rattle, or have jingles like a tambourine.

playing area

People play the duff in Spain, Portugal and North Africa. These drummers are Moroccan.

frame

Kalangu

skin

cords

hooked
stick

shoulder
strap

The kalangu is a talking drum from Nigeria. It can make different high or low sounds, like a human voice. The two drum skins are joined together by long cords. Musicians squeeze the sides of the kalangu in and out to make the drum beats higher or lower.

The kalangu is held under the arm and played with a hooked wooden stick.

27

Tenor drum

The tenor drum is often part of a military band. It looks like a snare drum, but its sound is deeper and it has no snares. In a marching band it hangs by a strap from the player's left side. It can also be part of an orchestra, where it rests on a stand.

In a marching band, tenor drum players twirl their sticks as part of the display.

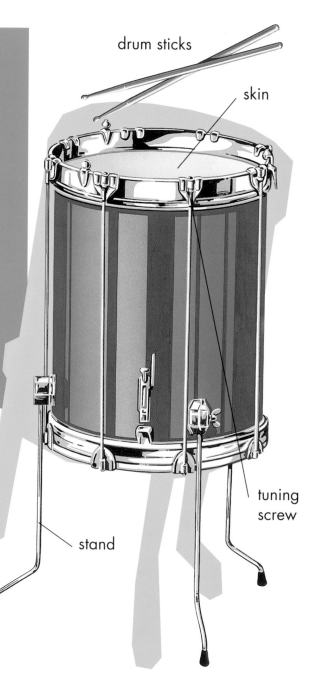

drum sticks

skin

tuning screw

stand

Atumpan

The atumpan is from Ghana. It is shaped like a large barrel, and rests on a wide stand. The skin is held tightly in place by cords tied around pegs. When atumpans are used in pairs they become talking drums. One drum sounds high, the other sounds low.

skin

cord

peg

barrel-shaped body

This performer uses a pair of hooked sticks to play a set of two atumpan drums.

Words to

accompany To play music alongside a singer or another player who has the tune.

beat The steady pulse of the music.

beaters Sticks of wood or wire used to hit or strike some instruments.

bowl The round, deep body of a drum.

brace A piece of wood, metal or pottery that joins together two different-sized drums, for example a pair of bongos.

cord A thin piece of rope, or twisted pieces of string or silk.

family (of instruments) Instruments that are similar to each other.

flautist A flute player.

frame A narrow band of wood on a small drum. The skin is stretched over the frame.

friction stick A thin stick or reed which is placed against the skin of a friction drum.

head The part of a drum that is struck. It is also called the skin.

heel The part of the palm nearest the wrist.

jingles Pairs of thin metal discs that make a bright jingling sound when shaken.

kettledrum A large drum in an orchestra. Kettledrums are also called timpani.

marching band A group of musicians who play military music as they march along.

remember

musician Someone who plays an instrument or sings.

orchestra A large group of musicians playing together.

pellets Tiny balls of metal, wood or other hard material that are attached to the cords of a pellet drum.

performer Someone who plays or sings to other people.

pitch How high or low a sound is.

rattle An instrument that is shaken to make it sound.

rhythm A rhythm is made by the beat of the music, and by how long and short the notes are.

skin The part of a drum that is struck. It is also called the head.

snares Metal wires that rest against the lower head of a snare drum. They rattle when the drum is struck.

solo A piece played or sung by one player or singer.

strike To beat (a drum).

talking drum A drum that makes higher or lower notes when its skin is made tighter or looser.

tuning paste A black paste that is smeared on to the skins of some drums. It makes the drum sound crisp and clear.

tuning screws Screws that can be turned to tighten or loosen a drum skin until it sounds the right note.

vibrations Very fast wobbling or shaking movements. Drum skins vibrate when they are struck.

Index